stars

DANIEL HUGHES

ashes & stars

Edited by Mary Hughes

Foreword by Edward Hirsch

Introduction by Michael Scrivener

WAYNE STATE UNIVERSITY PRESS Detroit

10 09 08 07 06 5 4 3 2 1

Library of Congress Cataloging-in-Publication Data

Hughes, Daniel, 1929–

Ashes & stars / Daniel Hughes ; edited by Mary Hughes ;

foreword by Edward Hirsch ; introduction by Michael Scrivener.

p. cm.

Poems.

I. Title: Ashes and stars. II. Hughes, Mary, 1931– III. Title.

PS3558.U35A6 2006

811'.54—dc22

2005031898

∞

Grateful acknowledgment is made to the College of Liberal Arts and the Department of English at Wayne State University for their generous support of the publication of this volume.

Designed by Elizabeth Pilon

Typeset by Maya Rhodes

Composed in 12/16 Berkeley Oldstyle Book

Contents

Foreword ix

Introduction xiii
Michael Scrivener

I

I Whip Around 3

If We Let Go, Of Course Death Has Us 4

Back 5

Icarus 6

At Last 7

Please 8

"The Book Fell from His Hand" 9

Take the Big Subject: Exile 10

Travel 11

Torn, Filthy Maps 12

Narcissus (Caravaggio) 13

I Have Lived 14

Nature 15

Frond 16

I Have Been Wrong, Wrong, Wrong 17

Even 18

Not Seeing Vermeer 19

II

To Charles Harte, Not Alive When Heaney Won the Nobel Prize 23

Why Didn't You Tell Me You Were the Great Poet's Muse? 24

Mother from Beyond the Grave 26

Soft 27

Next Time 28

Self-Wounding 29

Obituaries 30

Steve: The Silences 31

Anywhere Out of the World 34

III

To Mary 5:00 A.M. 37

Hurt 38

Glimpse 39

Best Choices 40

O I Like 41

You Feed Me 42

The Steady-On Agnostic Needs a Muse 43

Epipsychidion Again (To Karen) 44
To K—— 45
Let It Out (To E.W.) 46
Your Dead Lovers 47
Easter 1996 48
The Divine Sparks Trapped in the World 49
Were I 50
It's All 51

IV

Saint Mary's Schoolyard 55
Lament of Goliath 56
My Brutal Face Has Lasted Four Hundred Years 57
Painting Destroyed: Caravaggio 58
Berlioz Killed an Opera in His Head 59
Down 60
To a Poet 61
The Fate of Books 62
Poem 63
Reading a Writer Recently Dead 64
Not for Poets 65
After All 66
My Poem Making Its Way in the World 67
Here Come the Notes to My Poems 68

Foreword

He is survived by a welter of words.

Daniel Hughes

The poet Daniel Hughes, a radiant presence, left behind an enormous hole when he died in October 2003, at the age of seventy-four. He lived the majority of his adult life in Detroit, where for twenty-four years he had been a professor of English at Wayne State University. I would say that Hughes was deterred but not defeated by the debilitating illness of multiple sclerosis, from which he suffered for forty years. All through his illness, he lived a pure life of the mind. Art—English Romantic poetry, Renaissance Italian painting, European classical music—was for him a kind of religion.

Hughes and I taught at Wayne in the late seventies and early eighties. I have vivid memories of meeting him on the top floor of State Hall—first on his cane, then on his walker, finally in a wheelchair—and stopping to talk about poetry. He was a marvelous Shelley scholar, and the Romantics were always our touchstone. All his life he pursued the figures of Romanticism—what he calls here "the long chase of the Romantics"—with a kind of wild personal zeal. He took the deepest lessons of Romantic poetry to heart. He was an adept of Emily Dickinson's work. He also loved Robert Lowell's poetry and had been good friends with John Berryman. Indeed, Berryman's dream song #35, "MLA," was dedicated to Dan and his wife, Mary, and I often used to call out the first stanza when I saw him:

> Hey out there!—assistant professors, full,
> associates—instructors—others—any—
> I have a sing to shay.
> We are assembled here in the capital
> city for Dull—and one professor's wife is Mary—
> at Christmastide, hey!

The poem ends on a delicious note—"forget your footnotes on the old gentleman; / dance around Mary"—which I felt should be our theme song. Sometimes my conversations with Dan about poetry were so intense they had to be continued at his apartment in Palmer Park, which vibrated with the sound of opera blasting from the stereo. We also pored over art books and dwelled for a while together in the Italy of the mind.

Daniel Hughes published four individual collections during his lifetime—*Waking in a Tree, Lost Title & Other Poems, Falling,* and *Spirit-Traps*—which were distilled and gathered into *You Are Not Stendhal: New and Selected Poems*. This posthumous work, *Ashes & Stars,* may be his finest individual collection of all. His poems are filled with crafty ironies and witty refusals, with exact and exacting observations about the disappointments of life in a fallen time, yet they also present us with a singer who slipped through the side door onto the main stage and sounded the flaming, reckless, operatic notes of high splendor.

One of my favorite previous pieces, the poem "Too Noble," strikes a characteristic chord:

"Too noble," Rick said,
so we shut off the Beethoven
but still the sound
lingered about us, and lifted us
above the croissants and the jokes
we tried before we were awake.

No one's noble now—
we thought of the death of words, the slipping,
the history of disappointment,
but the sound stayed, as though the walls
claimed it.

We went for a walk in the bright morning.
The air was clarified, renewed, noble.

Hughes's poems often begin in disappointment but end on a note of noble attainment. It is as if the poet needed to overcome his own ironies to reach the state of rapture, which so called him. He needed to be lifted up. In "The Problem with Bliss," for example, he wonders if "bliss" was "one of those words gone forever."

But Campbell used it, the Upanishads use it,
and you ache toward it and speak it to yourself,
its sibilants rowing you out to the egoless sea.

Daniel Hughes's final work shimmers between the earth and the sky, between the grayness of ashes and the brightness of stars. One feels in reading him both the downward pressure of mortality and the upward swell of transcendence. Reading these last poems, I recognize that my old friend had a kind of epigrammatic mortal wisdom. He also had a spark of divinity in him. He believed that poetry itself could not be slain by time, and his own poems are filled with what Shelley called "our best and happiest moments . . . arising unforeseen and departing unbidden." He will be much missed, though his spirit lasts. It is inscribed in poetry.

EDWARD HIRSCH

Introduction

Michael Scrivener

When I saw Dan Hughes at Providence Hospital that Sunday in early October 2003, he was eating chocolates, reading the Sunday *New York Times,* and making wisecracks about George Bush. I did not expect him to die early Tuesday morning. Time, a central theme in his final poems ("old Time works us over"), had taken him from us, and no one felt that it was the right time. He had struggled mightily with a cruel illness, multiple sclerosis, for forty years, and it finally had won in the sense that it killed him, but the illness never killed his imagination, his wit, his intelligence, his dark humor, or his splendid poetry—five volumes of verse. In the many times we talked, from our first meeting in 1976 to our last, he infrequently talked about his physical health. In his poetry, including his final poems, he addresses some of the effects of his illness, but always mediated through images and figures that make his own victimization ("Please"), dependence ("You Feed Me"), exile ("Take the Big Subject: Exile"), and immobility ("Icarus," "Travel," "Torn Filthy Maps") participate in the general conversation of Western culture. He and his wife, Mary, handled the illness with astonishing courage. When people visited Dan and Mary on Friday afternoons—at a point when it was almost impossible for him to leave the apartment—the discussion was of art, literature, politics, music, and academic gossip, but only rarely the illness; it usually was not allowed to intrude on the conversation, although we were all aware of the unpleasant and rude guest who would never leave even when ignored.

Dan Hughes was born into an Irish Catholic family in Dover, New Hampshire, in 1929. He attended a Catholic school until ninth grade, then a public high school, and afterward he earned a bachelor's degree at the University of New Hampshire. He was working on his master's degree in English at Brown University when, during the Korean War, he was called into service as an ROTC officer in the army, where he served in an intelligence unit in Japan. Returning to Brown, he finished his master's, earned a doctorate in English, and taught until 1964, when he came to Wayne State University and taught until his retirement in 1988. In addition to his poetry, he published scholarly work on Shelley, Blake, Tolkien, Bellow, and Nabokov. His essays on Shelley, which were anthologized and frequently cited, earned him an international reputation as one of the foremost critics on the formal aspects of Shelley's poetry. He described how Shelley's verse worked as poetry, as language, and no one previously had explained such workings with so much eloquent precision. My own connection with Hughes began with those remarkable Shelley essays several years before we actually met in person. The preface of my dissertation on Shelley pays tribute to only a few critics, one of whom is Hughes.

As accomplished as he was as a scholar and critic, he cared more for his poetry, publishing his first book, *Waking in a Tree* (New York: Clarke and Way), in 1963, followed by *Lost Title & Other Poems* (Providence: Copper Beech Press) in 1975, *Falling* (Providence: Copper Beech Press) in 1979, *Spirit-Traps* (Providence: Copper Beech Press) in 1985, and *You Are Not Stendhal: New and Selected Poems* in 1992 (Detroit: Wayne

State University Press). This, his sixth volume of poetry, continues in the epigrammatic style he perfected over the years. It is not easy to locate Hughes's poetry, and I will use two axes to do so: American poetry and English Romantic poetry. The concentrated expression of these fifty-five poems, with their usual three-part structure—assertion, complication/negation/reversal, resolution—is reminiscent of Emily Dickinson, a poet he loved—see his "Not for Poets"—and whose work was always on a table near his chair in the living room. The many poems in this volume dealing with mortality also suggest Dickinson, a fellow New Englander with whom he shares an inventive, witty, and wry but unsentimental perspective on death. The epigrammatic style of William Bronk is also something like Hughes's style, but Bronk is far more abstract than Hughes. The objectivists—Zukovsky, Reznikoff, Oppen—had a superficially similar style, but the place played by objects in their work is played in Hughes's by ideas. One cannot read through Hughes's oeuvre without noticing the impact of Yeats and Lowell, especially on Hughes's first two books. The conflict between imagination and actuality, reflection and action, is a Yeatsian theme we find in his earliest and latest poems. It is not so much the confessional aspect of Lowell's work that one finds in Hughes, though there is some of that—"Funeral Home" and "The Millionaire's Son" are good examples of that style in previous volumes, "Mother from Beyond the Grave" and "Soft" in this volume—but one feels the pressure of Lowell in the way Hughes's Mediterranean poems are shaped. Lowell's imagination goes beyond the present moment for its centers of clarity—in the American past, in the European past. Hughes's imagination finds its bearings in his Europe, in Caravaggio, in Bach, in Greek myth. The here and now, the locus of energy for the poets in the William Carlos

Williams line of influence, is a point of departure for Hughes, something to reflect on, somewhere to leave and return to, but only occasionally to dwell within for imaginative inspiration. Similarly, the poetic forms in these final poems—quatrains, tercets, irregular sonnets, irregular rhymes—suggest the disciplinary rigors of high modernism, not the voice-centered poetics of the Whitman-Williams tradition.

Another impression one takes away after reading Hughes's work is the pervasive influence of the English Romantics. It is easy to forget that when Hughes was a young man becoming a poet and a critic, the poets he loved—Shelley, Blake, Byron—were scorned by T. S. Eliot and the New Critics as sloppy thinkers and sentimental poets lacking the discipline and formal mastery to merit consideration as first-rank writers. Like Harold Bloom, all of whose works he read carefully as they came out, Hughes championed the Romantics at a time when they were devalued by the dominant literary voices, and he remained committed to them to the end of his career. One of his final poems, "Best Choices," expresses vividly his Romantic sensibility.

> You, of course.
> And then the long chase of the Romantics.
> But I did not "choose";
> if that means to plan out, to plot.
>
> Oh, no.
> The fever bursting, the heart boiling,
> the secret sure ascension,
> words and bodies, talking, never still.

The Romantics make their presence felt also in Hughes's poetic Italy, the Italy of Byron's and Shelley's exile. Like Browning's Fra Lippo Lippi, Hughes in his poetry loves the world, its pleasures, its beauties, its available satisfactions. In the witty poem "Next Time," Hughes explains, "I would find the beauty in morality / next time." In this time, in his time of living, an erotic poem such as "O I Like" expresses the sexual intensity of the best experience as it is actually lived, not as it might be lived. In "I Whip Around" the poem's speaker "enjoy[s] both" Bach's praise of God and Montale's ironic star ashes, thus containing within the poem two different perspectives on temporality. The verb "whip around" is a wonderfully direct way to express immediate pleasure in two kinds of beauty; he wants both and will have both—no one is going to stop him. A poem like "Back" shows a Blakean fierceness in its insistence that the "sun within" is not inferior to the "sun without," both being "unreachable, / delirious, savage, and slain by Time." There is a Shelleyan tone in the wonderful poem "Even," Hughes's poem of faith that reminds us of Demogorgon's words at the end of *Prometheus Unbound:* "to hope, till Hope creates / From its own wreck the thing it contemplates." Hughes's poetry is very much of the contemporary moment in its urbanity, but it is also Romantic in its passionate intelligence.

The poems in this volume were written between 1994 and 1998, the oldest poem being an elegy for his friend and fellow poet Stephen Tudor, who visited Hughes weekly and typed his handwritten poems until his tragic boating accident on Lake Huron. After Steve's death, Hughes's friends and fellow poets Elizabeth Sokolow and Carol Kaplan took over the task of turning his handwritten work into typed texts he could revise. Most of the poems here were written in 1996 and 1997.

When I visited him, Hughes was always excited about something he was reading—a new book of poetry by John Ashbery, the latest from Harold Bloom, a new novel by Bellow. As his illness worsened, he rarely left his apartment, leaving if at all in an ambulance for a medical emergency. The life of the mind meant everything to him. "We hunger for the startlements, / we thirst for the smiling, distant water." It was Dan Hughes's way of being in the world that he found those startlements, startlements one finds again and again in his exactingly honest poetry.

part I

I Whip Around

"Ashes of the stars," says Montale.
But Bach says, "Praise God in every land!"
And I whip around enjoying both.
Wait for the slow movement,
wait for the exuberant end,
wait for the ashes to come down.

You have been there,
you stay on here;
this range, this vast stretch of time,
has you somewhere in it.

If We Let Go, Of Course Death Has Us

Assassin behind the rock,
monster bolting from the sea,
beast in the poisoned bush

which is why a closed fist is the best style,
which is why bent low is the surest method,
which is why we pass the dark fords carefully—

except yesterday, when I opened my arms,
and the fading blossoms like bruises
covered my body,

and I heard the thunderous petals falling.

Back

If I just back off,
the sun, lion-face, will float within,
O the steady burning then,
curly-head, come home to settle.

You rolled me to the park;
we bumped harmlessly forward.
You said, "See, the sun without
is like the sun within, unreachable,

delirious, savage, and slain by Time."

Icarus

Not that one,
played out by the poet and novelist
and advertising man.

But mine does not fall,
mine does not disappoint the father.

He sits there, whoosh, whoosh,
his wings making a terrible flutter,
a pathetic disturbance,
a laughable launching pad.

You may come upon him in the forest;
he wants to get out of there
and cause the scorching catastrophe.

But he sits there, arms akimbo
and weeps.
he contributes not one spark
to the destruction of the world.

At Last

Long the murdering thoughts,
slow and delaying,
and when you strike, school's out
and no one is helping or praying.

Did the Fates gibber,
and how can you grasp the schemes?
Who, *me*? Caravaggio's Matthew pointed to himself;
yes, you with your tacky dreams;

and that Man entering the room
may be Saviour or may be death,
but all's changed to clarity and call,
and your old life matters not at all.

Please

Please, no more songs of damage,
no more reaching into ruins.

We have heard this many times
and all is suspect, all is doubtful.

No one is free of broken masonry within.
Rock back on your heels, sparrow up.

I watch the heavy doors swing out,
oh, the greensward in the brain!

The romping, the remembering,
some feather falling on me.

"The Book Fell from His Hand"

Classic. And elegant.
and profoundly literary.
The Faerie Queen? *Jerusalem*?

It wasn't *The History of God;*
nor was it *God: A Biography.*
It was a book of names and addresses

entered in his now unreadable hand.
Never of much use before,
but for the first time

heavy on his heart.

Take the Big Subject: Exile

Take the big subject: Exile.
And not to hear from the emperor,
and not to be told from Florence:
"Your enemies are dead. Come home."
And not to pack your bags
or return on the red-eye.

I am sick of Guelfs and Ghibellines.
I've had it with Caesars.
Take the arrows as you always have.
How sleepy they make you,
over what plains they bear you.
Did soul throw out body,
or body point the wrong way?

Friends wait at the airport.
They are ready to support you and sustain.
They write the dark, exilic sentence
across your heart:
neither here, neither there.

Travel

Escaping, life is escaping.
Go ahead, O friend, tell me how
the Carracci in Bologna "flawed" your trip.
How wonderful the rest must have been.
Tell me about crumbling cathedrals,
and tell me about the deep water you flew over.
The Enormous Other outside your cabin.

My brain's an ax I broke on myself,
mad Dominican brained again.
And then the dazzling worlds,
and then the dark fulfillment.

Torn, Filthy Maps

Torn, filthy maps,
I've always hung them
and watched them disintegrate on the wall.

Italy, you say, Bavaria,
these were folded in my mind.
O poor desperate places,
curling up, unattended, unready,
their once-proud cities fading.

It hurts. It's what's left.
They are still in their places.
I have no longer any way to get to them.

Narcissus (Caravaggio)

I did not think I would be lonely;
I did not think looking into Styx,
I would be this pensive and sad.
You, viewer, enjoy the light on my knee,
but it only guides me to destruction.
Perhaps someone waits, perhaps someone pursues!
The transformations only tremble.
I am drawn in, not out of self-love,
but by a steady, low, nagging boredom,
the reflection of myself over and over
into water too shallow for me to drown in.

I Have Lived

Sixteen years longer than Rilke.
What for, howl the caverns.
Does it mean you can start now?

Counting is stupid.
Comparing is stupid.
Rilke's bad press cannot help you now.

Nothing can. Practice to live better.
Tear off the armor, drop the shield,
you, a warrior? Be slaughtered then

for one adamantine quatrain,
for a rhyme you abandoned long ago,
for one word mumbled by a nun.

Nature

Water and wood and stone!
Some people feed on them with happy hungers
and become water, and wood, and stone.

Lie back, feel the changes dissolve you.
You are mostly water, old soak,
your mind's a block of wood.
But never your heart a stone.
Too many disappearing, too many absent,
but never your heart a stone.

Frond

O lives puttering alone,
the book, the promotion, the leaving . . .
Has an angel with a frond
leaning from a cloud
put in your hands the cool touch of transcendence?
You could climb up on it;
you could touch it and burst into flame.
Look up as you topple over and the ground grabs you.

I Have Been Wrong, Wrong, Wrong

Only the Gnostics say otherwise
and when I rise in the mornings
the bells, the light, the curtains,
the sound in the street, the doorjambs shout
"You are wrong, wrong, wrong and this day is
another day of misapprehension and loss!"
Aren't you tired of being wrong and wrong again?

I am. Which is why I think of Valentinus
of Egypt, preaching in Rome.
He never said I was wrong.
He left space for me, he eased the father,
he saw the Sophia transformed
who does not shout at me
but goes through the day at my elbow,
speaking soft words:
"Watch out for the potholes,
I don't think you're wrong."

Even

Even no god is god.
How could it be otherwise?
This dank leaning, this flutter up
is a god.
Always out of you,
hail the pristine studies,
enjoy the simple rain.
Yearning is a god,
nostalgia is a god,
the door opens, and the woman coming in.

There are no names for it but god.
There are no signs of it that are not god.
I need the name and the word of it,
the day declining, the lid of night closing.
The only name for it is god.

Not Seeing Vermeer

That girl, in earring and turban,
is half a-tremble to see us.

Miranda! I shouted, and she turned,
hoping we were a brave new world.

We hunger for the startlements,
we thirst for the smiling, distant water.

I see what you look like now, dear, forever.
Keep turning toward us

expecting that something will turn up
for us all.

part II

To Charles Harte, Not Alive When Heaney Won the Nobel Prize

Yes, you would have swaggered a bit,
and mocked yourself a bit,
and been Irish beyond limits.

But you *were* Irish,
though, God! born in London
which you pretty much kept from us.

I think of your pleasure in it,
of your voluble bringing of the News,
and we would have drunk over it,
and mocked the others who have won,
except for Beckett and Yeats.

I miss the increase of your knowing
I want to share, now, this high-wishing thirst
with no one but you.

Why Didn't You Tell Me You Were the Great Poet's Muse?

Poets make so much of so little,
and I, the fumbler, uncertain still,
settled for your expression:
"God's rough notes for Paradise,"
and a glass of wine that I imagined
you urged toward me.
You were kind,
you saw me try to look Italian.
Twenty years later, I read you were the Muse,
the occasion, the source of poems.
Source is a word like a deep dream.
I missed your death,
I even missed the poet's passing
despite my morbid rapt attention.

Now you live in his poems
and he still makes your absence present,
a deep tangle of life,
the hard encounterings.

It's in the words that come and go,
it's in the statement you did not make:
"O, yes, I was the poet's Muse."

[Irma Brandeis was Montale's Clizia.]

Mother from Beyond the Grave

Your intense highly wrought envelopes come no more,
and the blue clear hand and the fever of information
and the ***detail*** that I spurned are gone too.
I'd like to know again what story you would choose,
in all of your excited, now receiving news.

Soft

My father, the undertaker, in his soft-shoe dance
nimbly at the door with his bright smile.
I saw him this morning and heard the patter and the slide
and understood at last what was meant by soft shoes.

He would get through life that way and leave no bodies behind
him,
only bury them until he tired
of those puzzled or familiar faces looking at him.
And retired early. And danced away.

Next Time

I would like the soy sandwich
next time.
I would find the beauty in morality
next time.
I would see through the gross flattery
next time.
I would change my life
as the poet says I should
and put my head back on my shoulders
next time.

Self-Wounding

No one can do it so fully,
no one can cut so cleanly,
your own guillotine,
and all the others with heads intact!

It increases the splendor of isolation,
it hurries on mortality,
it is never questioned by anyone.
You did it to yourself.

And now the day settles in
with incredible lucidity
in a high, bright glare
that shows your faint shadow on the wall.

Obituaries

Reading of the deaths of the good people,
their work with the poor, their contribution to society,
their lifelong altruism and selfless concern,
what can I ever say for myself?

A bother, a demand, helplessness incarnate!
He never lacked for others to do his work.
When you saw him, you knew what you must do.
You know you could never leave him alone.

He is survived by all not done.
He is survived by a swamp of feeling.
He is survived by a shadowy handful.
He is survived by a welter of words.

Steve: The Silences

1.

Don't fall out of heaven, Steve,
seeing how bad we are!
But, this is one poem
you won't print out for me,
so how will we know anyway, any longer,
what we're up against?

You'd smile and partly reject
comparisons with Hart Crane and Shelley,
but drowned poets make a chorus
in their deeps, final, thundering,
gathering to flood.
Break over us,
wash us now,
generous presence, dear friend.

2.

I wish I were somewhere away,
there to meet you,
far from events, clatter, misfortunes, the Dark Gaps,
and in you'd come as always,
and the high casual talk would begin.

9:30 and you don't call
2 P.M. and you don't come;
the task is mine and no one guides my hand
like that seductive boy in Caravaggio's *Matthew.*

I've always known,
I've always expected some gigantic demand,
and now the words splinter away,
mocking themselves, hating themselves.

3.

"Don't do this," you say. "Not this.
I'm not an excuse for poetry.
Learn about flowers, birds, tools,
the moods of the Great Lakes, the body.
Don't sit there pretending at redemption.
Is your life so thin, so bookish?
Do you think you'll get me back
in this frail casket?
    O Huddler with the worm,
    I had so much life to live
    and this is just poetry,
    paltry, poor nude thing I loved."

4.

Enormous, threatening, flaring,
this bad silence of my life
has deafened me for speech.

I know the great traditions,
but not mighty Milton or calm Herbert serves.
Should I cry then? Whom should I accuse?

It was life we had all along,
and this is not life,
and we will never know what it is.

And we will never return to name it.

July 1994
[For Steve Tudor, 1933–1994]

Anywhere Out of the World

Though the guitar lasts long and the woman is lovely,
I want to go anywhere out of the world
as my friend falling from his high sail
dove out of one world into another,
and wherever he went,
it was not here,
but where
the whelming eyes of the steady lake
wept to see him coming.

part III

To Mary 5:00 A.M.

Fierce against the consoling cliché,
wary of the vapid optimist,
you rise each morning in sorrow and dismay.

How long can you last, clear-eyed,
as old Time works us over?
It's allegory after all, darling.

And a wicked river god pulling us under.

Hurt

Hurt yourself by helping me,
the awful savage tyranny
of bodies now worn and cowed.

Do you remember? Once they were otherwise,
easy with each other, flowing—
bodies answering and proud.

Glimpse

Imagine if everything were something else!
Your lips, I mean, your hands, your breasts,
always yourself but this nagging glimpse
that, by God! changes are going on.

I know too many books and pictures.
I know the history of doom.
How we started in the ancient days,
how we found our way to this room.

Best Choices

You, of course.
And then the long chase of the Romantics.
But I did not "choose";
if that means to plan out, to plot.

Oh, no.
The fever bursting, the heart boiling,
the secret sure ascension,
words and bodies, talking, never still.

O I Like

O I like the briny taste of you.
It smacks of origins, deep Time, sources,
the self as snail—holding on furiously.

Yes, keep the social woman others see,
keep the mask, I live in the grotto of you,
water lapping at the entrance, the vapid sun quenched.

You Feed Me

You feed me.
Whoever thought the job

so formidable,
the tasks so unending.

And I mean food,
and I mean the looks

when our eyes fix together
and feed there too,

seeking insights,
seeking signs.

Then the awful hunger
when you're away

and there's no feeding then,
not one morsel or crumb.

The Steady-On Agnostic Needs a Muse

And not himself, and not his deep procedures,
and not the research swimming in—
not Marcus Aurelius, Julian the Apostate,
and not the sex-defeated theologian,
Wow! heels off the floor, bumping on the ceiling,

you dear, dressing, undressing,
looking out, looking in.

Epipsychidion Again

TO KAREN

It's not you, dear; it's Time.
Old Butcher Shop, old hands
working us over in the meat market.
A novelist I knew preferred his muse ugly,
in gunboots, overalls, crossed eyes.

It was his way of protecting himself.
Yes, I did study the poem;
yes, I see you in it,
and the fainting and the failing,
and the delirious island—
were perfect for 1960,
old Butcher Shop yet to come.
But then, the hot, cool place, the flameout
and my unembarrassed gaze.

To K——

Of course, I would like to hear.
Come up to me, trailing your stories.
The decades apart, the blind, wan hopes.
What we once expected of each other!

If you come now, weary and worn,
I will let you in with wary cries;
let fall on us the whole faraway thunder.
Not bad we'd say, touching like nervous deer.

Let It Out

TO E.W.

Let it burst out!
From what?
Stop starting on the far side;
take that girl forty years ago
in her blue uniform, her blonde hair
falling over her collar—did it say U.N.?
Were you too distracted to take in the Nations?

Always the pale transformer,
always the hunter of events
with bags begging to be filled;
she didn't want to be stuffed inside;
she probably had
another life to lead.

Your Dead Lovers

Do they weigh on you?
How do they weigh on you?
I want the full, lascivious information.
I want the detail of bone and breath and position.

I have no good intention in this matter.
I have an almost sneering curiosity.
How does it feel now? Wistful? Melancholic?
Or is it all the spirit of your later life,
the dark, orgasmic night receding?

There is no honor in my asking—
there is only a ragged self-interest, and worse,
a frantic knocking for you to let me in.

Easter 1996

I thought the resistance would be total.
I no longer understand you, I no longer
think you will come to me with the ciborium.*

Don't fight these dated images.
You came to me with a secret sharing,
yes, you did, on your clothing, in your heart.

I paint myself because I can't afford models.
I paint you because I keep losing you.
I paint us so we will live forever.

*Any vessel designed to contain the sacred bread or wafers for the Eucharist.

The Divine Sparks Trapped in the World

Of course. But do we release them or keep them?
When you came home, I felt both functions,
the one outward, soaring from throat to head,
the other belly-bound, renewed, sinking down
to that invisible place where they lie on the bed.

Were I

Were I to go on,
I'd like to make a myth of you;
if we were to go on,
I would consult the legends.

What? that naked-nude shabby pair,
and the avenging angel confident above!
I thought his name was Time;
he said he was Time as he forced us away.

It's All

It's all underground music now—
the catch in the throat, the wobble,
and never the high notes ascending,
but always the gray sounds of trouble.

Did you think I was a tenor
who might cushion the grave?
Not even a bass, not even a singer,
not even a sound marked by a stave.

part IV

Saint Mary's Schoolyard

You bastard who twisted my arm,
and made me buy you cigarettes—
how did I get the others to beat you up?
How did I get them to descend on you?

Was it pity, was it my Sebastian look?
I'm sure it happened; I remember the kids' revenge,
my first and only day of power.

No wonder I've led a Franciscan life,
no wonder I've withheld my commands;
watch my penitent words hold the page.

Lament of Goliath

Always to fall like all your hopes and plans.
Yes, I built there, yes, I challenged him,
but they always love little David
with his accurate sling and curly hair.
Don't think I didn't work hard to get there;
don't say my power was all brute and boasting.
His foot is on my neck; my head is sliced away.
It was a good head,
full of plans for the nation.
It was a growing head
smarter each day with giant thoughts.
I can't think them anymore;
you have lost a great bloody thing.

My Brutal Face Has Lasted Four Hundred Years

I'm the executioner on the right
in *Salome Receiving the Head of John the Baptist*
and the torturer on the left in *The Flagellation,*
and all the time you have been shuddering at my face
—cruel lips, sneering eyes, shot hair—
know, I was just a guy in Naples trying to get by.
I did not see that face in the morning,
I did not see that face in the bay when I looked in;
I never thought I was anything special.

He did. And now my face has lasted so long,
you might come to find it almost lovable.

Painting Destroyed: Caravaggio

The angel guides the hand of the illiterate saint
and shows his lovely body through the thin shift.
It's what you need to get started today:
an angel to stand by your desk

and kiss your ear and direct your hand
and offer his body in carelessness.
The church disliked the saint's jutting foot
and cardinal Uptight hated the angel
who shows how close inspiration is to sex.

God had it bombed out of existence in 1945.

Berlioz Killed an Opera in His Head

Berlioz killed an opera in his head.
He thought of the squabbles, the expense, the resentment,
and the endless Parisian indifference,
and the years of contention and despair.

At dawn the themes came, the characters
rustled forward, coughing, adjusting their clothing—
for a moment he heard the glorious opening theme
and the love music, leaner now than in *Romeo and Juliet*.
He sat down again; he went back to bed.
Berlioz killed an opera in his head.

Down

“Bulldozed in the middle of the night,”
the great old Art Deco building disappeared.
I know, I know, and the morning of empty lots,
the vague yearning spaces, the dark gaps
took hold and we wandered in the rubble,
our inner soft fallings still sounding at noon.

To a Poet

You can't have my City,
baking in the noon of missed chances,
its gods and saints contorted inside,
trembling to meet the fevered tourist.

It's mine, despite the thousands who come through.
It's mine, behind my right eyeball
throbbing like my long disease:
a weight, a splatter, a loss you don't want,

a calamity you can't have.

The Fate of Books

So long in their neglect,
so chaotic in their placing,
so deep in their nostalgia—
what can they do but explode!

They all want someone turning them,
they all bear the stains of remembrance,
they all suffer their dark youthful purpose

which was to explode!

The easy, the only way to get rid of them,
scorch in the brainpan,
avalanche in the heart.
Oh, the billion words blowing away!

Poem

I roared into the classics;
I stuffed Bulfinch down;
I broke into the Bible,
with all those stories strewn.

You see me here expanding;
what conflicts, what rich dismay!
Don't think me narcissistic—
the Not Me's born today.

Reading a Writer Recently Dead

It was an extreme way to get my attention.
You might have been on my reading list,
one of your books might have been hiding here,
your name could have jumped from an old review.

But now we're both in for a serious moment;
me, because I want to see what you have left,
you, because your work is hung with crepe;
it will not be added to or changed again.

These pages then have a new solemnity.
I open them. I hunt. I stiffen.
The words are little beaky mouths,
crying: "Listen to me, heed me, hold me,

let this book be a bomb in your hands."

Not for Poets

Not for poets.
Good, I hate their cliques,
their mutual scratchings,
their poses, their vast conceit.

Not for poets.
But, O, gulp, who else listens
to the hum, spots the strategy,
lives in *slantness*?

Except poets.
See them bend over silence,
ears dirty with the page,
hearing themselves, hearing you.

After All

How awful that poetry is character after all—
which is why you
grope for the guide
to lead you from the dark word
to the one good verb,
your first and last chance.

My Poem Making Its Way in the World

Well, it's out there;
it must be going somewhere;
it marches up and knocks on someone's door.
But knock's the problem.
It's out there like an exhalation;
it's out there like a sound forgotten three days ago.
You were passing from room to room to room and heard something!
Not the sound of shields on the ancient plain;
not the prophet's burly dark command.
Listen again. Recall it. Keep it on hand.

Here Come the Notes to My Poems

Not UPS, not the post office,
not the carriers over mountains,
not the dead pigeons cried over by women,
not wild mountain monks of Magnasco,

but slender, pinched figures with battered briefcases,
holding the information away from themselves,
with a small disgust—they have come now,
and at last we can understand each other.